I AM. I DO. I WITNESS.

BECOMING A HEALTHY CHRIST-FOLLOWER WHO INSPIRES A HEALTHY MOVEMENT.

JACOB MATHEW

To,
Neena, Josiah and Joash
and
The AGK Family in Kolkata
For
Making Jesus Famous

Contents

Contents

First Word

Martin Luther is perhaps the best-known leader of the 16th century Protestant Reformation which marked a crucial turning-point in the history of the Jesus Movement. The Church had been going through a period often described as the `Dark Ages' – a period in which the gospel of Christ had become grossly commercialized. Sincere church-goers were led to believe that a person could be assured of a place in heaven through the purchase of `indulgences' [cash payment for eternal spiritual benefits].

Luther's reading of the Bible resulted in God opening his eyes to the true way of salvation in Rom 1:17- ...*the just shall live by faith* and a powerful, life-changing conversion experience. It's a truth reiterated and made explicit in Eph 2:8-9, that followers of Christ all over the world hold close: *We are saved by grace through faith...not by works!* Luther's conversion and subsequent propagation of this truth led to a massive movement which became known as the Reformation, for which he is most widely known.

Unfortunately, a fact that is less known is that Luther's discovery of that great truth led him to overemphasize it to the exclusion of another vital truth affirmed in scripture – that *faith without works is dead* [Jas 2:17-26]. Since this was an important emphasis in the book of James, Luther tried to undermine and dismiss it as "an epistle of straw". Despite the great reformer's criticism, thankfully, James remains an integral part of our New Testament. As is widely acknowledged today faith and works are not opposed to each other but - rightly understood –are closely linked in a root-fruit relationship: faith is the root of which works are the fruit.

Luther's emphasis, however, continues to dominate much of the thinking within some sections of the faith community. This has sometimes resulted in an unhealthy dichotomy amongst Christ-followers seen in a damaging disconnect between our profession of faithand lack of authenticity in our lifestyle. It is in this context that Dr Jacob Mathew invites us to take a fresh look at James' letter through the lens of a three-pronged, holistic framework which he views as a prescription for healthy discipleship: *I Am* [God-shaped Identity]; *I Do* [Christ-like Lifestyle]; *I Witness* [Spirit-led Mission].

This book is a creative, vividly imaginative and highly readable summary of the message of James' epistle. It is also an earnest invitation from a thoughtful pastor for Christ-followers of this generation togrow out of a superficial `lip-service' faith into healthy mature disciples.But more than that, it is a passionate call from the heart of one who longs to see [in his own words] "...a greater movement of vibrant fresh flourishing genre of healthy Christ-followers" emerge in this generation.

The author is a pastoral colleague, a winsome fellow-pilgrim and a dear friend, but it's not for those reasons that I warmly commend this work to the reader. I do so because this work is not just a well-crafted, captivating piece of writing - it's the overflow of a life of authentic Christ-followership – the truths he expresses with such creativity here...I see him living out each day! That's perhaps the main reason this book is a must-read...we don't see enough of that in the Church today, do we?

Dr. Ivan Satyavrata
The Assembly of God Church
Kolkata, India

FIRST WORD

Playback

Most good things are accidental. Or Coincidental. But usually God-orchestrated.

Well, that is the story of the formation of this book. When I was invited to speak at the Calcutta Keswick[1] last year, my immediate response was, 'NO'. I felt too unqualified to fill the shoes of the reputed and experienced speakers who have spoken at this annual event over the years. However, my reluctant 'YES' opened the opportunity for me to reflect deeply on one important question:

What are the vital ingredients of a healthy Christ-follower?

This reflection led me to the Book of James. And the rest is what you find outlined in this book.

But, I would need to backtrack a bit. In 2015, I got into a doctoral study program that opened my eyes to rediscover my faith journey at a deeper level than I had imagined possible. I discovered that faith was more than just spontaneous, impulsive steps towards God. Faith had a faithful framework. A holistic structure that could help you significantly impact your world. This framework is embedded into this book.

I guess I would need to playback further. My last twenty-five years is a story of great friends and wise mentors. Friends who shaped my life. Mentors who shaped my call. Who I am and what I do is a work-in-progress of their influence on my life. Informal conversations and learning moments with these friends and mentors have ingrained priceless values and principles in my life. These values get fleshed out in this book.

If I playback just once more. I start at the beginning. The first twenty years of my life. My family. My parents and my brother. They formatted almost every aspect of spiritual and life formation in my life. My church family. Lots of God-encounters and people-encounters fine-tuned how I perceived my faith journey. The formatting and the fine-tuning process is deep-rooted in this book.

This playback journey is to distinctly clarify that almost everything in this book is not original. It has the imprint of people who have influenced me. Precious people who are God's gifts to me. They have modelled for me what it means to be a healthy Christ-follower.

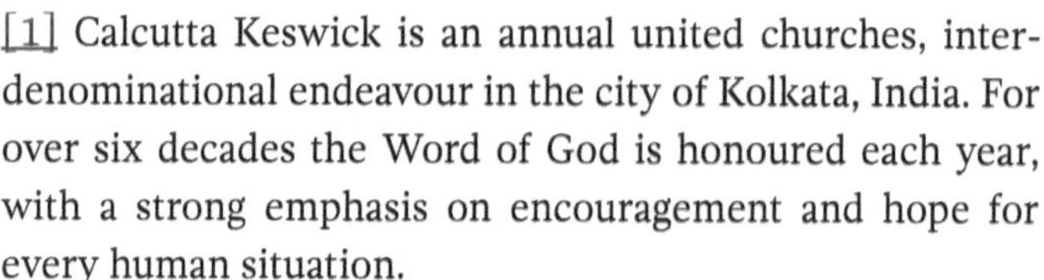

[1] Calcutta Keswick is an annual united churches, inter-denominational endeavour in the city of Kolkata, India. For over six decades the Word of God is honoured each year, with a strong emphasis on encouragement and hope for every human situation.

The Journey

Introduction: Famous Five

In late 2019, my Senior Pastor's wife, Sheila Satyavrata, gifted a fishbowl with five fish inside to my two sons. Our boys were delighted and there started the journey of nurturing fish at home. More than fourteen months later (through the Covid-19 lockdown of 2020), through countless water-changing experiences, fish-feeding moments, ambience-adding items, the fishbowl remained the same. Unfortunately, every few months there were new fish in the bowl as the old ones seemed to die regardless of all our passionate planning outside the bowl.

After a lot of self-evaluation and reflection, I discovered the secret to why these fish didn't seem to last long in our fishbowl: **Unhealthy conditions.**

The conditions of the fishbowl were unhealthy and not conducive to grow a movement of fish. Maybe I was putting the wrong fish together, or not giving enough oxygen, or not showing enough care. Maybe they don't like the songs I sing.

For your information, I went into therapy with close pastoral colleagues who are experts at fish management. Just kidding.

But today, we are preparing to navigate life in a post-pandemic world. As we revaluate our faith, community and the Christ-movement, we as leaders, and often all of us as the family of believers, have given greater focus and concern to have a neat good-looking fishbowl. The externals all seem great. But we wonder why there doesn't seem to be a greater movement of a vibrant fresh flourishing genre of healthy Christ-followers. To put it plainly: why does it seem around the world, and across

India, and here in Kolkata, 'the fish are dying' or 'we are dying'?

The reason is simple: *unhealthy conditions.*

I am inviting you to a conversation based on the Book of James called *'Healthy Follower, Healthy Movement'.*

How can *I* be a healthy follower of Christ?

How can *we* become a healthy Christ-movement?

The Book of James paints an interesting landscape of the unhealthy conditions he discerned as influencing the Jewish Christ-followers in the first century. The context, audience and background information of this letter is worth looking at more closely.[1]

James presents very interesting imagery which is important to understand the environment of his readers. When we understand these images, we become more observant of the church context today. It is also a convicting reminder of the immediate painful scenario around us in the twenty-first-century Jesus-movement.

There are five caricatures that James places before us. Caricatures of the generation (then and now). There are different categories of people within our church community. These are the famous five that causes problems all the time. The famous five that destroy our health and the health of our movement.

1. Mirror-watchers

Those who hear and don't act are like those who glance in the mirror, walk away, and two minutes later have no idea who they are, what they look like (James 1:23-24 MSG)

We may look at God's word for a long time but refuse to obey His Word as soon as we turn our eyes away from it! All we require is a split-second to forget the mirror of God's Word.

2. Seat-assigners

If a man enters your church wearing an expensive suit, and a street person wearing rags comes in right after him, and you say to the man in the suit, "Sit here, sir; this is the best seat in the house!" and either ignore the street person or say, "Better sit here in the back row,"(James 2:3 MSG)

Our job is to assign seats for people. We assign people based on personal preference, bias based on colour, caste, race, community, and a thousand other things that divide the world. Seat-assigners are everywhere. In politics, business, educational institutions and within the church. Seat-assigners have the power to divide churches and entire nations.

3. Fire-starters

In the same way, the tongue is a small thing that makes grand speeches. But a tiny spark can set a great forest on fire. (James 3:5 NLT)

We can be called fire-starters; ship-rudders; a bit of a horse; but the most powerful imagery is a forest on fire. As fire-starters with our 'tiny tongue', we can change the world. We exist everywhere. One loose tongue is all that is needed to mess up the beautiful unity.

4. Calendar-planners.

And now I have a word for you who brashly announce, "Today—at the latest, tomorrow—we're off to such and such a city for the year. We're going to start a business and make a lot of money."(James 4:13 MSG)

We set the agenda and we know we are in control of our world. We are the boasters. We will boast about it all and nobody can stop us.

5. Gold-grabbers.

Your gold and silver are corroded. The very wealth you were counting on will eat away your flesh like fire. This corroded treasure you have hoarded will testify against you on the day of judgment. (James 5:3 NLT)

We are constantly searching for ways to be rich. We will do whatever it takes to grab gold.

When we look at these characters, we immediately tend to be like the nominal believer who came to church on a cold winter morning. There were just about five people in the church. The pastor preached his heart out with a strong message of commitment, especially delighted that the nominal believer was there to hear this strong message. At the end of the service, the nominal believer came and hugged the pastor. The pastor was almost in tears imagining that his hard message had had its desired impact. Until the believer opened his mouth: *Pastor, that was a very powerful message! I wish those lazy hypocritical people were here to listen to it.*

The Jesus-movement in the first century and the twenty-first century confront the same issues. The famous five are everywhere:

Mirror-watchers –*Disobedient followers*
Seat-assigners – *Prejudiced followers*

Fire-starters –*Divisive followers*
Calendar-planners – *Selfish followers*
Gold-grabbers – *Power-hungry followers*

What is it going to take for the next generation of the church to look beyond the fishbowl and provide healthy conditions that will spearhead a healthy Jesus-movement?

If you are:

- a *home-maker* who faithfully attends your church on a weekend: this call is for you.
- a *young man or a young lady* grappling with understanding the significance of Jesus in a 21st century post-modern world: this call is for you.
- a *young professional* wanting to make a difference in your workplace: this call is for you.
- a *sincere seeker* seeking to understand who Jesus is: this call is for you.
- a *pastor or leader* longing to go beyond the external features of faith and ministry: this call is for you.

How are we going to be healthy followers who can with God's blessing grow a healthy movement?

How am I going to go beyond the fishbowl and seek to cultivate healthy conditions that will not just bloom my life but multiply my influence on an entire generation?

This book is going to be a conversation where we are going to look at three critical elements that are going to be crucial for us as individuals if we are going to be healthy followers.

The book of James doesn't mince words but bluntly and candidly places before us a challenge: *What will it take for us to be healthy Christ-followers?*

I am going to invite you, as you read this book, to prayerfully read the Book of James at least *twice*. I discovered it approximately takes about twenty-five minutes to read the entire book of James. My prayer is that in your private time alone with God, while reading God's Word alone, the Holy Spirit will speak to you in unique and unimaginable ways.

[1] There are excellent books and online resources which would provide a great opportunity to delve deeper into the context of the Book of James. Some of my favourites are:

https://www.biblestudytools.com/james/

https://bible.org/article/introduction-book-james

https://craigkeener.com/category/new-testament/james/

The IVP Background Commentary(New Testament) by Craig Keener

The Message of James(The Bible Speaks Today Series) by JA Motyer

Section 1: I AM

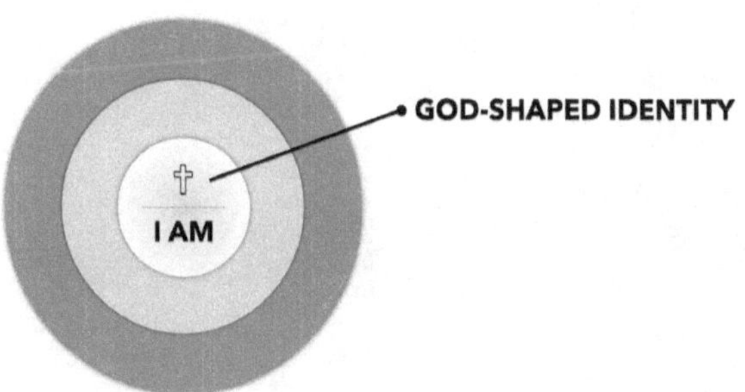

CHAPTER ONE

INTRODUCTIONS ARE IMPORTANT

Introductions are always important. It sets the tone for people to have the right expectations.

When a Swiggy[1] delivery boy comes and delivers your pizza or pasta at your doorstep and calls on your mobile phone: *I am Akram from Swiggy (or Tony from Zomato).* You don't expect anything more than a pizza that you paid for.

But suppose your phone rings and the person on the other side states: *Good evening I am Sriharsha Majety, the CEO of Swiggy; I am standing at your door.* The expectation immediately changes. Would he give anything more than a pizza?

It doesn't matter whether or not the CEO knows how to hold a pizza correctly. All that matters is that his position defines who he is.

Unfortunately, in the twenty-first century, our culture has shaped us to define people based on the position they hold, the achievements they have had, and the beautiful façade of their social media pages. *We watch the world through the lens of what people do instead of who people are.*

The first critical element of what it means to be a healthy follower is a *God-shaped identity*.

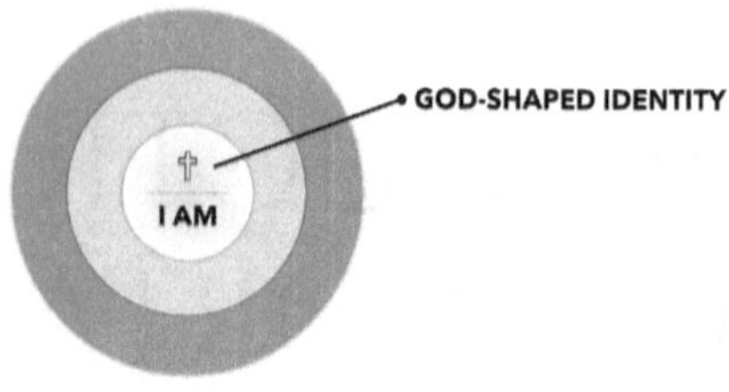

[1] Swiggy or Zomato are online food delivery companies in India.

CHAPTER TWO

WHO I BELONG TO SHAPES WHO I AM

I, James, am a slave of God and the Master Jesus...(James 1:1 MSG)

I, James,

You might say *pause*. Which James is this?

There are at least three James who could have potentially written this letter.[1] But, most scholars agree that the James who has written this letter could have actually pompously introduced this letter:

I, James, the 'actual' brother of Jesus

I, James, the chairman of the Jerusalem church

I, James, the apostle in the grade of Peter and Paul

But James uses this seemingly basic introductory greeting to highlight the most important feature of what it means to have a God-shaped identity.

Who I belong to shapes who I am

I am James, a slave of God.

My titles don't matter. My status doesn't matter. My achievements don't matter. All that matters is that I belong to God.

"Slave" comes from the Greek word *Doulos*. One who completely surrenders himself to the will and authority of another. It was used of one who sells himself into slavery to serve another. [2]

Some wanted to escape the bondage of hard masters, but others knew the kindness and love of their master's heart. The Law (Exodus 21) provided a way for them to remain as slaves to their kind masters. The slave could go to his owner and tell him that he wanted to remain a slave. The slave would then be taken to the tabernacle where the priest would lead him to the doorpost and pierced a hole into the lobe of his ear with an awl. From that time on he was the slave of his master. As an author eloquently stated, 'Wherever he walked, his ear proclaimed the character of his master.'[3]

James, in his opening comments, wanted to make it very clear: *I am James. I belong to God. Jesus is my master. Who I am is based on my Master's identity.*

That is a bold declaration, making it clear that he lives for the instructions of God.

An important question for us is: *Whose slave am I?*

Whatever or whoever enslaves me directs me and controls me.

Who I belong to shapes who I am. What is the evidence of whose slave I am?

- *My daily schedule is proof of whose slave I am*
- *My daily habits show whose slave I am*
- *My words reflect whose slave I am*

A slave loves the master and lives to please and impress the master at all times in all things.

A slave doesn't make his own agenda or plan out an alternative agenda for his day. He is waiting for the next instruction of his master.

Do I love Jesus?

Is Jesus my master or am I led astray by many masters?

Can I make this statement:

Jacob Mathew, a slave of God and of the Lord Jesus Christ?

Can you put your name down?

______ (Your Name), a slave of God and of the Lord Jesus Christ.

If not. Why not?

What are the things in our lives that cause us to disobey the master and run it the way we want it? Time to stop. Pause. Let go of everything that stands in the way of the Master's lordship over our lives.

One of the most stunning moments in the Bible is God's encounter with Moses in Exodus 3. Thus far, Moses had defined himself based on his life in the palace as Prince Moses or his life in the wilderness as Shepherd Moses. But in Exodus 3, he discovers: *his community doesn't define him. His case history doesn't define him.*

Moses is on his knees before the presence of God. Moses is face to face with the *I am that I am.* Moses discovers: *The Great I Am defines who I am.*

That encounter with God opened Moses' eyes. The final lap of his journey on earth (the final 40 years): *he lived as a man who belonged to God.* No wonder the scriptures record Moses as: *very humble—more humble than any other person on earth. (Numbers 12:3 NLT)*

My prayer for you today is that you will have a burning bush experience with God. An experience that will redefine who you are.

[1]   https://bible.org/seriespage/20-james-introduction-outline-and-argument

[2]   https://bible.org/seriespage/2-introductory-greetings-titus-titus-11-4

[3]   https://bible.org/seriespage/2-introductory-greetings-titus-titus-11-4

CHAPTER THREE

WHERE I STAND SHAPES WHO I AM

A young, successful couple found their dream home. Shortly after purchasing it, the couple sat at their kitchen table to enjoy a delicious breakfast. The wife looked out of the window, and to her surprise, she saw her neighbour hanging dirty clothes on the clothesline.

'Those clothes are not clean, they are still dirty!' she said to her husband. 'Someone needs to teach her a thing or two when it comes to washing her clothes!'

A couple of days later, the couple sat down at their kitchen table for another meal. The wife saw her neighbour hanging clothes on the clothesline. But this time something was different.

'Wow, look!' the surprised wife said to her husband, 'Her clothes are clean! Someone must have taught her how to wash her clothes!' Without raising his head from his plate, the husband kindly responded, 'Actually, honey, I got up early this morning and washed our window. It was dirty.'

James presents in his letter the value of standing in the right place to experience the fullness of all that God has created you to be. *When you are in the wrong place you get the wrong picture. When you are in the right place you discover who you are and who God created you to be.*

Dear brothers and sisters, when troubles of any kind come your way, consider it an opportunity for great joy. For you know that when your faith is tested, your endurance has a chance to grow. So let it grow, for when your endurance is fully developed, you will be perfect and complete, needing nothing.

If you need wisdom, ask our generous God, and he will give it to you..

God blesses those who patiently endure testing and temptation. Afterward they will receive the crown of life that God has promised to those who love him.".

"He chose to give birth to us by giving us his true word. And we, out of all creation, became his prized possession. (James 1:2-8; 12-18 NLT)

Standing in the right place has nothing to do with standing on top of the Burj Khalifa or in front of the Taj Mahal and taking a selfie.

V. 2: *When troubles of any kind come your way, consider it an opportunity for great joy.*

James presents to us the value of standing in the face of the worst storm: *'When troubles come your way...'*

But, how do we stand in the face of your worst storm? *'consider it an opportunity for great joy'*

It is almost like taking a selfie with a huge smile on your face when you are surrounded by the worst storm in life!

Recognize that God shapes you best to be all that He has crafted you for in your worst storm. Your identity as a healthy Christ-follower is formed best when the enemy lands his worst punch on your face.

v. 4 – your endurance is fully developed, you will be perfect and complete, needing nothing.

In a sense, James is stating you will be complete and perfect like your master Jesus – the awesome model of who you should be like – when you stand up where you are and refuse to quit in your worst pain.

Where I stand shapes who I am.

Where should you stand? James seems to present a few clues of where you should stand. If you refuse to budge you will be shaped more and more into God's amazing identity.

- **Stand strong in your worst trial**

For most of us, 2020 was possibly the worst test we have ever faced in our lives. Pandemic. Cyclone Amphan (those of us in Bengal, India). Lockdown. Those irritating masks. The million hand-washing exercises.

In the midst of it all:
Stand still. Don't quit

- **Stand strong in your faith**

Don't let go of your faith. Under any circumstances.
Yes, your faith will be tested. Yes, you will be pushed to the corner and tempted to give up your precious faith.
In the midst of it all:
Let go of everything else but hold on to your faith.

- **Stand strong in God's wisdom-**

James 1:5 is a favourite verse that we would like to give to students preparing for their school examinations.

If you need wisdom, ask our generous God, and he will give it to you.

Sometimes it works, if they have prepared well for it. Here, James is talking about something bigger than just an exam question paper. He is talking about this painful scenario when you are facing your worst trial. Your faith is feeble and weak. You are facing a dead-end. You have no idea or clue. No way to escape. Don't be tempted to make foolish choices. Stand strong and depend only on God's generous wisdom. He is always faithful.

If you stand in God's wisdom alone, you will make the smartest moves in life!

- **Stand strong in God's Word**

Even when nothing makes sense treasure the precious gift of His Word.

James 1:18 – He chose to give birth to us by the power of His Word.

Who Am I? He spoke His life into me and chose me to be His most priceless possession.

If I stand on the power of His Word alone – even when everything else shakes around me – I will be steady, stable and strong.

Where I stand shapes who I am. It all depends where you stand.

CHAPTER FOUR

WHO IS WITH ME SHAPES WHO I AM

Where do you think all these appalling wars and quarrels come from? Do you think they just happen? Think again. They come about because you want your own way, and fight for it deep inside yourselves. ...

You wouldn't think of just asking God for it, would you? And why not? Because you know you'd be asking for what you have no right to. ..

You're cheating on God. If all you want is your own way, flirting with the world every chance you get, you end up enemies of God and his way...

So let God work his will in you. Yell a loud no to the Devil and watch him make himself scarce. Say a quiet yes to God and he'll be there in no time. Quit dabbling in sin. Purify your inner life. Quit playing the field. Hit bottom, and cry your eyes out. The fun and games are over. Get serious, really serious. Get down on your knees before the Master; it's the only way you'll get on your feet. (James 4:1-10 MSG)

This passage uses three strong words to describe Christ-followers who are supposed to be healthy and strong and Christ-like. I guess you would be offended if anyone used these terms to describe you.

Adulterers
Sinners
Double-minded

James seemed to say - Hi guys, this is who you are! You showcase this identity as an adulterer, sinner, and being double-minded.

Just in case the original readers of the letter of James or you and I are offended with this thoughtless use of words against respectable people like us.

James makes it clear: *Who I am with shapes who I am.*

In this passage, he outlines three dangerous dimensions of our faith journey and how they are destroying us.

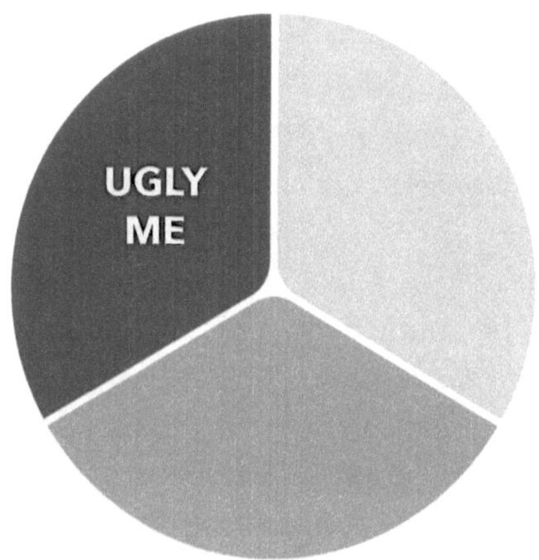

We have been grooming our **fallen nature ((v. 1-2 – 'the evil desires at war within you') –** *the ugly me*

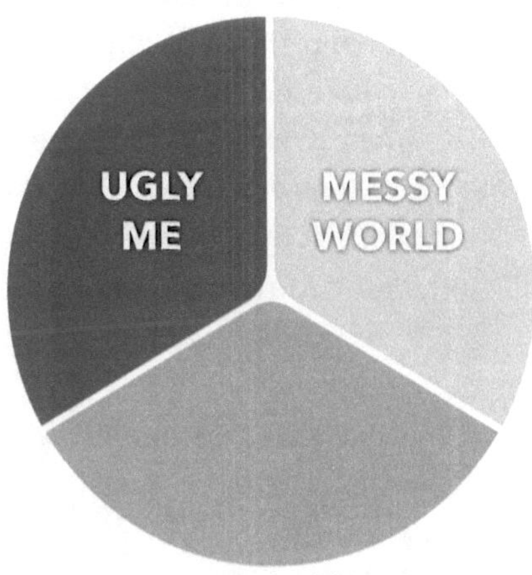

We have been flirting with the **world system (v. 4 – 'friendship with the world')** – *the messy world*

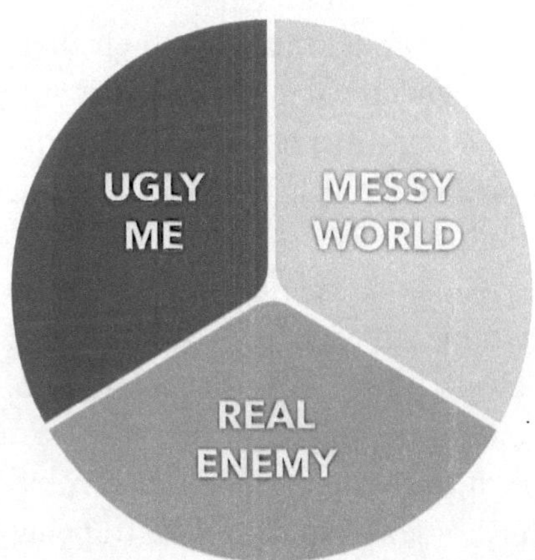

We have been toying with the **Devil (v. 7)** – *the real enemy*

The more we allow ourselves to be shaped by the 'ugly me', the 'messy world' and the 'real enemy', we showcase our identity to be an adulterer, sinner, and double-minded.

James sets the record straight in James 4: 4(NLT) *'Friendship with the world means enmity against God.'*

How do I escape from or win this nearly impossible battle against the fallen nature, the world system, and the devil?

You cannot do it at all!

Our daily battle is like a fish encountering the alligator-snapping turtle.

What am I talking about?

The prehistoric-looking alligator snapping turtle is the largest freshwater turtle in North America and among the largest in the world. With its spiked shell, beaklike jaws, and thick, scaled tail, this species is often referred to as the "dinosaur of the turtle world."[1]

They are carnivorous, and while their diet is primarily fish, they have been known to eat almost anything else they can find in the water—in a few cases even small alligators! The alligator-snapping turtle relies on a uniquely deceitful method of hunting for fish.

The turtle will lie completely still on the floor of a lake or river with its mouth wide open. At the end of the turtle's tongue is a small, pink, worm-shaped add-on. The turtle wiggles the end of its tongue so that it looks like a worm moving through the water. When a fish comes to eat the worm, the turtle's jaws rapidly close, trapping the fish so that it cannot escape.

Similar to the snapping turtle's lure, is our battle with our fallen nature, the world system, and the devil.

How can you have a God-shaped identity?

The only way is realizing:

There is no way out until you give up.

Trying on your own and totally give up.

This is a good response: *'Hands up! I surrender!'*

James 4:7(NIV) - Submit yourselves, then, to God

I like how the Message translation scripts it: *So let God work his will in you.*

You cannot do it. Only God can set you free from the dangerous and painful grasp of your fallen nature, the world system, and the devil!

No, it's not true that God enjoys watching you suffer under the controls of the enemy.

God is jealously longing to set you free. (read James 4:5)

I wonder if you are ever in a room with kids fighting over a remote control and the TV channel to watch. I have two sons and there are those moments – where both my boys want to watch different channels. One wants to see Masha and the Bear and the other one wants to see actual bears on National Geographic. Both of them are fixated and addicted to what they want to see and they have a huge fight grabbing the remote control from each other's hands. Daddy walks into the room and has the difficult job of grabbing the remote control and trying to put sense into their heads.

In the journey of life, *freedom happens the moment you hand over your life's controls to God alone.* You are addicted, distracted, and fighting to get the better piece of the world with the remote in your hand.

Sometimes, there are those unique moments when God is obsessively and jealously eager to set you free. He grabs the controls from your hands before you can destroy yourself.

Who I am with shapes who I am.

When I submit to God and I draw closer to God:

- *God's beautiful nature overcomes 'the ugly me' and grooms us to be like God*
- *God's Word sets us free from following the charms of the 'messy world'*
- *God captivates you at all times and the devil flees from you*

[1]   https://www.nationalgeographic.com/animals/reptiles/facts/alligator-snapping-turtle

CHAPTER FIVE

LIKE JESUS...

Once upon a time, in a Garden at the foot of a mountain, there was a group of men who had gathered. It was a late night. This group of men were quite tired and went off to sleep. Except for one man. Here was a man who was getting ready for the battle of his life. A man who was tempted in every way, suffered in all areas, but there was something different about him.

He recognized that he belonged to God.

That recognition made him pray even when he was at his weakest:

"Abba, Father," he cried out, "everything is possible for you. Please take this cup of suffering away from me. Yet I want your will to be done, not mine." (Mark 14:36 NLT)

I belong to you. I am willing to let go of my every desire.

He recognized that regardless of his worst storm: at the moment of death on the cross, he refused to budge and he decided to stand strong.

That recognition made him pray: *Father, into your hands I commit my spirit (Luke 23:46 NIV)*

He recognized that his daily relationship with God was his greatest priority.

That's why He prayed: *'Glorify your Son, so that your Son may glorify you'* (John 17:1NIV)

His name is Jesus.

He exhibited a God-shaped identity.

Today, the same Jesus is here with you. He is with you in your home or your office or wherever you are.

He took the lonely journey to the cross, so you can belong to God alone.

He was obedient to the very end to His father's voice, so you can stand strong and be faithful in the midst of your worst storm.

He died on the cross and rose again on the third day, so you can be set free from the power of Satan(real enemy), the messy world(the world system), and the ugly me(the fallen nature).

If you have not personally experienced this Jesus and allowed Him to be your saviour and Lord - I invite you to surrender your heart to Him and kick-start your journey to be a healthy Christ-follower.

You are precious to Him. He loves you. He wants to start a brand new relationship with you.

MY PRAYER

Dear Jesus,

Thank you for choosing to love me, giving your life for me, and for inviting me on this journey to follow you.

Thank you for dying on the cross for my sins. For rising again on the third day. Thank you that in you Jesus, I have hope, life, and purpose.

I surrender to your Lordship. I commit to being all that You want me to be.

In Jesus Name. Amen.

Section 2: I DO

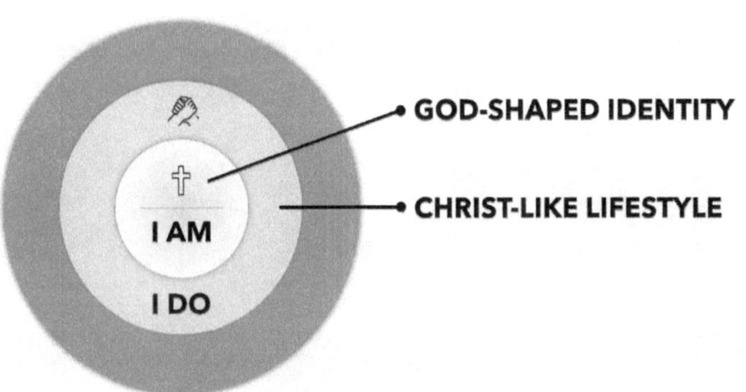

CHAPTER SIX

OUR LIFE'S GOAL

I wonder if you have ever heard about HD.

HD was very focused and committed and ambitious. He had worked hard for this day. He dreamt of reaching this pinnacle. He dreamt of climbing higher than anybody else. He wanted to be more famous than anybody else. Finally, the day arrived. He was seated where he always wanted to be. But just when he had arrived at the pinnacle of his success, he had a great fall. It was quite embarrassing and nobody could help HD at all. That's when I guess they sang these famous words:

Humpty Dumpty sat on a wall.
Humpty Dumpty had a great fall.
All the king's horses and all the king's men
Couldn't put Humpty together again!

An article entitled, *Corporate and Government Scandals: A Crisis in 'Trust' – Integrity and Leadership in the age of disruption, upheaval and globalization,* presents the painful reality of the twenty-first century world:

The lack of integrity (actual or perceived) in public office and the private boardroom is a critical reason we are now experiencing what has been described as a crisis in leadership and trust.[1]

Alan K. Simpson, famously said:

"If you have integrity, nothing else matters. If you don't have integrity, nothing else matters"[2]

Business, politics, entertainment, sports, or the church - the twenty-first century has revealed that unless WHO I AM and WHAT I DO is in alignment, we crumble inside regardless of how majestic our empire is.

Unhealthy movements are the result of unhealthy leaders.

An unhealthy Jesus-movement happens when we have unhealthy Christ-followers.

James expresses it explicitly, candidly, and bluntly: A Jesus-like lifestyle is critical to being a healthy follower.

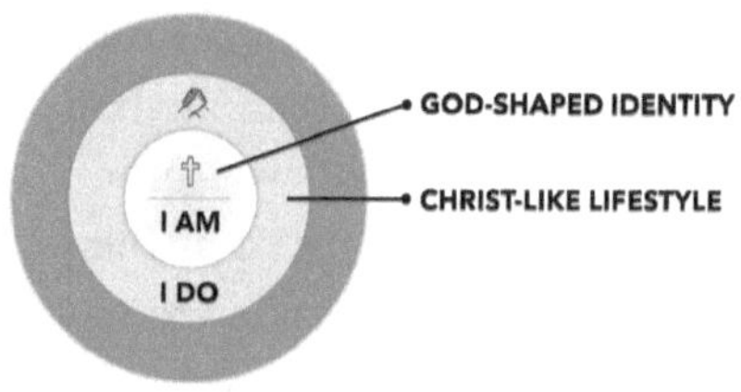

The more I read the Bible and the more I follow Jesus, I discover that my life's goal is pretty uncomplicated. It is simply this: *to become like Jesus.*

Well-known author and speaker, John Stott said it best towards the end of his life: *So, I want to share with you where my mind has come to rest as I approach the end of my pilgrimage on earth, and it is- God wants His people to become like Christ. Christlikeness is the will of God for the people of God.*[3]

What does it mean to 'become like Jesus'?

I, James, am a slave of God and the Master Jesus. (James 1: 1 MSG)

If Jesus is my Master, my life's basic goal is to be like Jesus in all that I do.

In the well-known book, In His Steps, Charles Sheldon places this powerful challenge before us: to ask ourselves this question before making any decision in our lives: what would Jesus do(WWJD)? Based on that book, in the twenty-first century, we have made it into an advertising blitz – WWJD t-shirts and wrist bands and banners.

The only problem with that challenge(as much as I love the primary intention): is that Jesus never studied in my college, handled a social media account, lived in my neighbourhood, lived next door to my neighbour or worked with my boss.

So I am really not sure what Jesus would do in my twenty-first century world?

But if I do study the gospels and meditate on the life of Jesus – I would discover – **What Jesus did do in His first-century world!**

One of my favourite books in recent times is *ReJesus* by Michael Frost and Alan Hirsch. It talks about rebooting your life with Jesus as the centrepiece of your life.

The authors state: *There is no truer way to encounter Jesus afresh than prayerfully cycling through the Gospels and asking God to give us fresh insight into the remarkable person we find there. We must give our hearts, minds, souls, to the One around whom history turns.*[4]

The more I choose to follow what Jesus did, the more I live a life like Jesus.

A Jesus-like lifestyle is the only antidote/only vaccine to an unhealthy Jesus-movement.

The more we have healthy Jesus followers who live like Jesus, the more Jesus becomes real in our world.

The world may have never read the Bible, or seen Jesus. But the more they see you, would they see Jesus more?

Our God-shaped identity must be fleshed out in a Jesus-like lifestyle.

Who I am must carve out What I do.

I am leads to *I do.*

Being and Doing is the heads and tails of our followership with Christ.

Lead like Jesus by Ken Blanchard, Phil Hodges, and Phyllis Hendry is a book worth reading to help you grow as a Christ-follower and leader.[5] The authors highlight the value of habits as those activities you do to stay on track with God and others. According to the authors, Jesus modelled two types of habits: Being habits and Doing habits. Being habits mean that like Jesus we make time to reload our energy and refocus our perspective by following: solitude, prayer, the study of God's Word, the application of Scripture to real life, and loyal relationships.

Doing habits mean that like Jesus we make time to share the Father's love to the community by showing: grace, forgiveness, encouragement, and community.

The Book of James is a DOING book that pushes us beyond the boundaries of just BEING and "staying-safe" faith.

You might ask me to pause at this point: and remind me that historically there have been some who have questioned whether the Book of James should have been included in the New Testament because of his overemphasis on doing. Are our 'good' deeds replacing the greatest act of Jesus on the cross? Isn't all our righteousness like filthy rags?

Some scholars even pushed further: Did you notice JESUS is mentioned only twice in the Book of James: James 1:1 and 2:1?

What kind of Jesus-lifestyle are we talking about, if Jesus is not even mentioned more than twice?

I think, for James, that's precisely the point! *Show your God-shaped identity by showing off your Jesus-lifestyle.*

Our faith is not just in displaying our rituals and traditions and religious jargons and the language of faith. Our faith is made real when we live like Jesus in our world.

In the Pentecostal tradition to which I belong, vibrant worship services and expressive times of worship with loud singing and spontaneous prayers are greatly valued. James wants me to go beyond my genuine faith moments expressed within a worship service and to live like Jesus when I step out of our worship service. *My loud singing inside is meaningless if outside the church service I practice a quiet faith.*

On a Sunday morning when you step outside your church, regardless of where you worship and the unique worship practices you follow – *you carry a Jesus-lifestyle into your world.*

I am reminded of a young boy who was intensely watching people pray in the church. Towards the end of the worship service, he went to the front of the church hall, knelt at the altar – and desperately prayed. The pastor of the church was really impressed with the boy's passion for prayer. But he was confused with the words of the boy's prayer – he kept repeating – 'Lord, One Foot down – One Foot down'. As the boy finished praying and got up to leave, the pastor put his hand on the boy's shoulder – 'Buddy, I was really impressed to hear you pray. But what did you mean when you prayed – one foot down'?

The boy replied 'Oh I was just telling the Lord that all these beautiful prayers, creatively rehearsed in their heads by all these people, that people were praying with their lips – should go one foot down from the head to the heart and they will start practising it'

The pastor himself, convicted, knelt at the altar 'Lord, one foot down.'

[1]   http://104.131.51.121/2017/05/31/corporate-and-government-scandals-a-crisis-in-trust-integrity-and-leadership-in-the-in-the-age-of-disruption-upheaval-and-globalization/

[2] Alan K. Simpson was the co-chair for President Barack Obama's National Commission on Fiscal Responsibility and Reform]. As quoted in Eyewitness to Power (2001) by David Gergen

[3]   https://www.cslewisinstitute.org/Becoming_More_Like_Christ_Stott

[4] Frost, Michael, and Alan Hirsch. *Rejesus: A Wild Messiah for a Missional Church.* , 2009. Print.

[5] Blanchard, Kenneth H, Phil Hodges, and Phyllis H. Hendry. *Lead Like Jesus Revisited: Lessons from the Greatest Leadership Role Model of All Time.* , 2016. Print.

CHAPTER SEVEN

EARS: HOW I LISTEN

James, in this short letter, presents before us five essentials on what it means to live a Jesus-like lifestyle. What it means to have a faith that is one foot down.

Each of these essentials is connected to five integral elements of our human body.

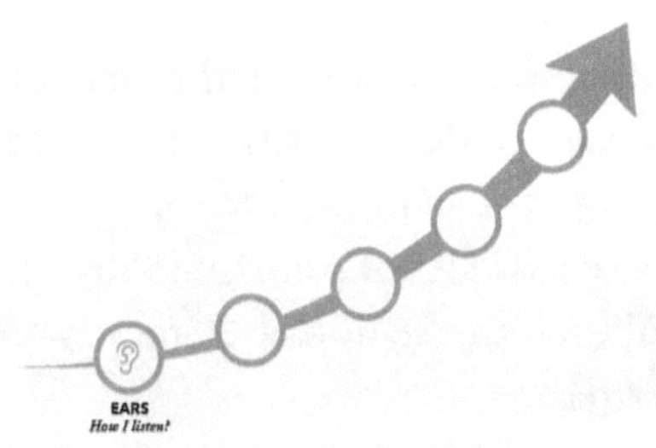

Ears – How I Listen

JAMES 1:19(NLT) 'Understand this, my dear brothers and sisters: You must all be quick to listen...'

The Jewish audience (the original readers of this letter) would be familiar with the instruction in the Book of Proverbs.

Proverbs 1:8

My child, **listen** when your father corrects you. Don't neglect your mother's instruction.

Proverbs 5:13

Oh, why didn't I **listen** to my teachers? Why didn't I pay attention to my instructors?

Proverbs 12:15

Fools think their own way is right, but the wise **listen** to others.

Proverbs 17:4

Wrongdoers eagerly **listen** to gossip; liars pay close attention to slander.

Proverbs 25:12

To one who **listen**s, valid criticism is like a gold earring or other gold jewellery.

The priorities of my life define how I listen.

If God is the most important priority in my life, then everything I listen to is filtered through this important framework: *How do these words that I have just heard, honour God in my life and my world?*

If loving people is a vital priority in my life, everything I listen to is filtered through -*how do these words help me to value people better?*

Our master Jesus demonstrates what it means to be quick to listen:

Jesus listens to a man late at night (John 3). He was quick to listen regardless of the inconvenient time-schedule.

Jesus listens to a lady at the well (John 4). He was quick to listen regardless of the case history of the person.

Jesus listens to a blind beggar's cry (Luke 18). He was quick to listen regardless of the status of the person.

Jesus listens to a dying thief on the cross (Luke 23). He was quick to listen regardless of his pain and suffering.

Jesus listens to two discouraged shattered men on the road to Emmaus (Luke 24). He was quick to listen and make personal time for just two people on a lonely road regardless of the historic public event of his resurrection.

How do I listen? I must learn to listen like Jesus.

One of my role models for being quick to listen is my wife, Neena. I have always marvelled how she can listen to people for countless hours - in person, on the phone and in recent times on Zoom calls. There have been moments where I have sat at a distance and wondered how one can be so undistracted, still, and focussed listening to a young person for several hours.

What the world needs are: healthy Christ-followers who will listen more and speak less.

Recent surveys have shown that Generation Z (young people born after 1996) is the loneliest generation ever.[1] There is a loneliness epidemic. This is shocking despite the fact that this generation has more tech tools and social media apps at their fingertips that help them to connect faster and more efficiently than ever before in history.

What they need most is one person to listen to them.

Will you be the one?

Quick to listen.

***

[1] https://www.cnbc.com/2018/05/02/cigna-study-loneliness-is-an-epidemic-gen-z-is-the-worst-off.html

CHAPTER EIGHT

EYES: HOW I SEE

*My dear brothers and sisters, how can you claim to have faith in our glorious Lord Jesus Christ if you favour some people over others? For example, suppose someone comes into your meeting dressed in fancy clothes and expensive jewelry, and another comes in who is poor and dressed in dirty clothes.If you give **special attention** and a good seat to the rich person, but you say to the poor one, "You can stand over there, or else sit on the floor"—well, doesn't this discrimination show that your judgments are guided by evil motives? (2:1-4 NLT)*

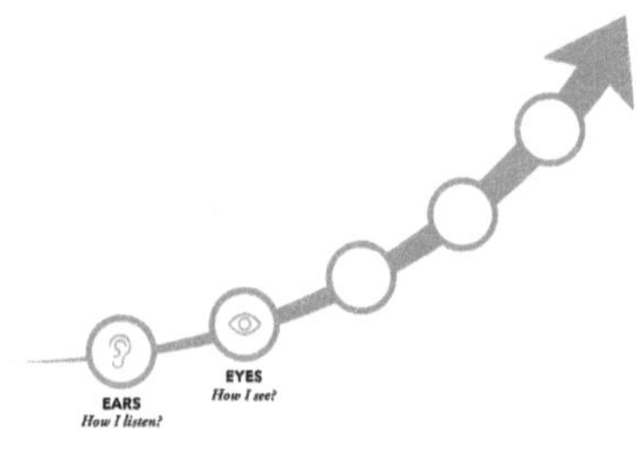

Eyes: How I See

All of us are always watching. But it depends on what we choose to see.

I am reminded of a young couple renting a vacation cottage for a week. One afternoon, the husband looking out of the drawing-room window at the swimming pool and exclaimed, "Darling, let us change our clothes and go get some exercise!" His wife, who was washing the dishes in the kitchen and looking out of the kitchen window watching some people play tennis, quickly agreed. While she dressed for a tennis match, he put on his swimming trunks!

The window you choose to look out at the world often determines what you see.

In James 2:1-4, the key standout phrase for me is 'SPECIAL ATTENTION'

The first century in the context of this letter: the rich got richer and the poor got poorer. This led to unpleasant discrimination against the poor. This was how the world operated in the first century. But the tragedy was that when people walked into a community or a location where the glorious living Jesus was to be worshipped and magnified, there was gross partiality and discrimination as some people got special attention while others were neglected.

In fact, in the first century, this discrimination often led to violence and war.

How I see the world should be based on how God sees me.

It would be wonderful if in the morning, when I look in the mirror, Jesus whispers to me: *You are God's creation. You are created in the image of God. You are valuable.*

Often we stop there. We build our self-esteem and carry on through the day. Only valuing our own identity.

Wouldn't it be wonderful if we carried this Jesus-whisper right through the day?

You step into your room and when you see your wife and kids (you continue this whisper of Jesus to your wife and kids): *You are God's creation. Created in the image of God. I value you.*

When you step out of your home and see your neighbour who belongs to another religion: *You are God's creation. Created in the image of God. I value you.*

When you get into the public bus and you see a shabbily dressed man who is stinking of alcohol (you continue this Jesus-whisper): *You are God's creation. Created in the image of God. I value you.*

When you reach your office and see your office colleague who belongs to another culture and speaks another language (you continue this Jesus-whisper): *You are God's creation. Created in the image of God. I value you.*

When you bump into your worst enemy in the office corridor (you continue the Jesus-whisper): *You are God's creation. Created in the image of God. I value you.*

It would be a beautiful world, if how I see the world is based on how God sees me.

It would be a beautiful world if all of us, as Christ-followers, carried this Jesus-whisper outside our church services and carried it into our world.

I wonder if you are celebrating your birthday today. If you are, happy birthday to you!

Or on the day you celebrate your birthday remember my special birthday wish to you!

Each of us has a date of birth. A date that signals our entry into this world. We record this date everywhere. Official documents and all kinds of online documents.

Do you know what is the importance of that date?

When you and I were born into the world as babies, go ahead and search any part of the body, we did not carry a brand: **MADE IN INDIA** (Or the country you belong to).

When you are born, you don't carry a brand of your nationality, religion, race, language, or caste. Your human body is branded with only one mark: you are born in the image of the living God.

Sometime after you and I were born, we added tags and brands based on what people told us. Today, we have the most divided world ever in the history of the human race because we believed the lies that we told each other.

George Floyd in 2020 was pinned down for nearly nine minutes and was murdered because of the colour of his skin.[1] Countless murders happen every day because of the choice of a person's religion or culture or language.

It's true. God sees everything. But there is some things God is blind about: *God is colour-blind, religion-blind, nationality-blind, caste-blind, and culture-blind.*

God gives special attention to everyone regardless of his background or history or culture.

If we have a God-shaped identity, a Jesus-like lifestyle leads us to see the world through the eyes of Jesus.

---

[1] https://www.nytimes.com/2020/05/31/us/george-floyd-investigation.html

CHAPTER NINE

TONGUE: HOW I SPEAK

.... For if we could control our tongues, we would be perfect and could also control ourselves in every other way.

⸱⸱ And among all the parts of the body, the tongue is a flame of fire. It is a whole world of wickedness, corrupting your entire body. It can set your whole life on fire, for it is set on fire by hell itself.

People can tame all kinds of animals, birds, reptiles, and fish, but no one can tame the tongue. It is restless and evil, full of deadly poison. (James 3:1-12 NLT)

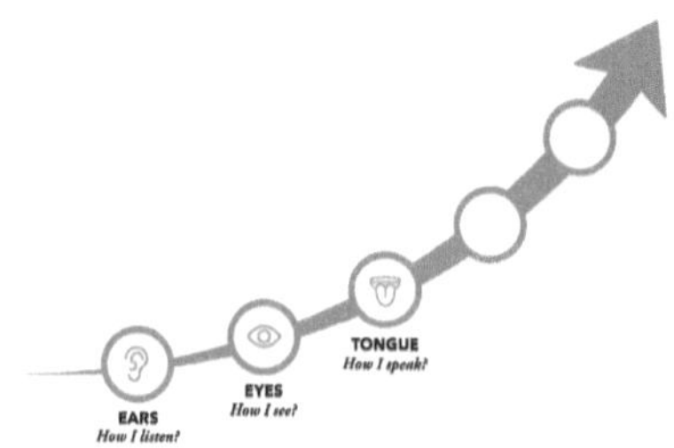

Tongue – How I Speak

Nobody knows who you are unless you open your mouth and speak. In the twenty-first century, we can restate it as: nobody knows who you are unless you send out a tweet!

One of the biggest causes of an unhealthy Jesus-movement in any part of the world is the unhealthy use of the tongue.

It can affect anyone anywhere.

Pastor in the pulpit who misuses the pulpit to abuse his members.

The deacon in the deacon board misuses the board room to abuse the pastor and the congregation.

A believer in the congregation who misuses his calling to abuse and divide the Body of Christ.

How can I speak like Jesus?

James 3: 12-18 places before us the only two options on who motivates our speech.

When our speech is motivated by the devil, it is full of bitter jealousy, selfish ambition, earthly desires, unspiritual thoughts and ideas, disorder, and evil.

When our speech is motivated by God and His wisdom, it is full of purity, peace, consideration for others, submission, mercy, sincerity, impartiality, and goodness.

The question before us is: *Who is motivating our speech?*

Speaking like Jesus means there are moments when you have to be silent and willing to be misunderstood.

One of my favourite passages in the Bible:

Then the high priest stood up before them and asked Jesus, "Are you not going to answer? What is this testimony that these men are bringing against you?" But Jesus remained silent and gave no answer. Again the high priest asked him, "Are you the Messiah, the Son of the Blessed One?" "I am," said Jesus.

"And you will see the Son of Man sitting at the right hand of the Mighty One and coming on the clouds of heaven."" *Mark 14: 60-62 NIV*

The greatest teacher of all time. Greatest leader. Greatest speaker about whose sermons more books are written than anybody else in history. Jesus.

But Jesus placed in court and asked to defend himself. He remains silent.

He did not need to defend Himself. He was absolutely confident in who He was and what God wanted to do with His life. Nothing anybody does or says can change who He is.

Jesus practised the rare response of silence, even when He had all the right to speak up and defend himself. Yes, he was not always silent; he did speak up later in response to another question.

How about myself? When I feel offended by others' words about me or when I feel the need to defend myself to PROVE WHO I AM?

In an era of fake news and self broadcasting and hashtags, our silence is not the easiest thing to do, because all that is within us is tempted to speak up and prove that we are right.

How about practising silence like Jesus and trusting God to set things right?

It is said that, on a lonely hill in an English country churchyard stands a colourless, grey slate tombstone. The old-fashioned stone bears an epitaph not easily seen unless you stoop over and look closely. The faint engraving read:

<blockquote>
Beneath this stone, a lump of clay,
Lies Arabella Young,
Who on the twenty-fourth of May,
Began to hold her tongue.
</blockquote>

Let me not wait until my death-date to hold my tongue.

HANDS: HOW I ACT

Dear friends, do you think you'll get anywhere in this if you learn all the right words but never do anything? Does merely talking about faith indicate that a person really has it? For instance, you come upon an old friend dressed in rags and half-starved and say, "Good morning, friend! Be clothed in Christ! Be filled with the Holy Spirit!" and walk off without providing so much as a coat or a cup of soup—where does that get you? Isn't it obvious that God-talk without God-acts is outrageous nonsense? (James 2:14-17 MSG)

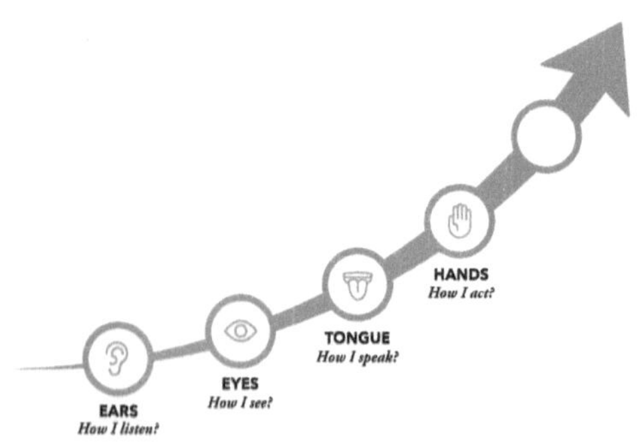

Hands – How I Act

God-talk without God-acts is outrageous nonsense.

Listening like Jesus. Seeing like Jesus. Speaking like Jesus. They must lead us to act like Jesus.

James outlines the basics of how we should act like Jesus with our hands.

What I powerfully speak with my lips must lead to how I sincerely act with my hands (v. 14-17).

Great faith plus genuine action is the secret to healthy Christ-followership (v. 18-24).

Quiet faithful action honour God more than loud empty faith (v. 21-26).

Abraham and Rahab. Both of them quietly obeyed God. Their acts of faith led both of them to becoming heroes of faith in Hebrews 11.

I am reminded of the familiar story often quoted by John Stott of the pastor to whom a homeless lady turned for help, and who (no doubt sincere, and because he was busy and felt helpless) promised to pray for her. She later wrote a poem and sent it to him.

I was hungry ... and you formed a humanities group to discuss my hunger.

I was imprisoned ... and you crept off quietly to your chapel and prayed for my release.

I was naked ... and in your mind you debated the morality of my appearance.

I was sick ... and you knelt and thanked God for your health.

I was homeless ... and you preached to me of the spiritual shelter of the love of God.

I was lonely ... and you left me alone to pray for me.

You seem so holy, so close to God ... but I am still very hungry – and lonely – and cold.[1]

Do my God-acts match up with my God-talk?

~

[1] Stott, Dr J. R. W, Roy McCloughry, and John Wyatt. *Issues Facing Christians Today.* , 2011. Internet resource.

FEET: HOW I LEAD

Look here, you rich people: Weep and groan with anguish because of all the terrible troubles ahead of you. Your wealth is rotting away, and your fine clothes are moth-eaten rags...For listen! Hear the cries of the field workers whom you have cheated of their pay. The cries of those who harvest your fields have reached the ears of the Lord of Heaven's Armies.

You have spent your years on earth in luxury, satisfying your every desire. You have fattened yourselves for the day of slaughter.You have condemned and killed innocent people, who do not resist you. (James 5:1-6)

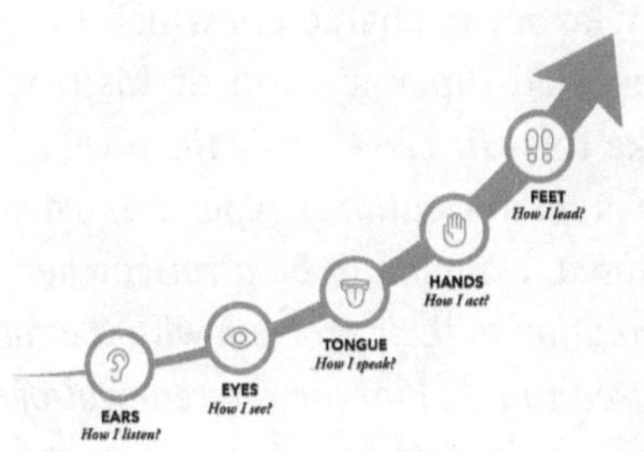

Feet – How I Lead

If I ask you a question: Are you a leader? Most believers and even some leaders would act humble and push back: *I am not a leader... I am just a nobody.*

The reality is that you and I, and every one, our feet are going somewhere. And somebody is following us somewhere.

Our steps in the right or wrong direction are leaving footprints for the next generation to follow.

It all depends on where our footprints are going?

In James 3 and James 5, James specifically – talks about three kinds of leaders:

- Teachers who teach and influence a generation with their supposed words of wisdom.
- Rich people who have the financial resources to shape the economy of a generation.
- Employers who have the capacity to grow a generation of better employees.

But James indicates that in each case, these leaders used their power and influence to destroy the next generation.

How I lead will determine the health of the next generation.

One of my favourite characters which I read for my son is the famous Pied Piper. Fiction or history, the familiar story goes like this- *In 1284, while the town of Hamelin was suffering from a rat infestation, a piper dressed in colourful red clothing appeared, claiming to be a rat-catcher. He promised the mayor a solution to their problem with the rats. The mayor in turn promised to pay him for the removal of the rats. The piper accepted and played his pipe to lure the rats into the Weser River, where all but one drowned. Despite the piper's success, the mayor went back on his promise and refused to pay him the full sum. The piper left the town angrily, vowing to return later to take revenge. On Saint John and Paul's day, while the Hamelinites were in church, the piper returned, dressed in green, like a hunter, playing his pipe, and in so doing attracting the town's children. One hundred and thirty children followed him out of town, where they were lured into a cave and never seen again.*

Two crucial and convicting lessons that I remind of myself every time I read this story:

- **How I lead shapes younger leaders** - a leader (the mayor in this case) who was not a good role model for a younger leader (Pied Piper).
- **Hurt people hurt others**- the younger leader (Pied Piper) who followed the leader to be a bad role model and destroyed an entire emerging generation.

If I am a healthy Follower, I set the tone for a healthy movement.

How I lead will influence an entire generation.

CHAPTER TWELVE

LIKE JESUS...

Peter is face to face with Jesus. Peter had messed up. Betrayed Jesus three times.

Almost gave up following Christ. Was all set to go back to his fishing profession.

That's when Jesus shows up. After breakfast, Jesus asks Peter this most pointed question: Peter, do you love me more than these?

Thrice Jesus asks Peter: Do you love me?

Peter broken and shattered, but glad to be reconciled to His master and friend: Yes, Lord, you know that I love you.

Jesus: Feed my sheep.

This is a unique conversation between Jesus and Peter.[1] It was as if Jesus was telling him: Peter, I am going to start a new story with you. It's time to burn up the old storybook of betrayal, mess-ups, and bad choices. I am starting over with you. If you love me, I am about to start all over with you. Listen to me. Look at me. Speak for me. Be my hands. Be my feet.

Today, regardless of where you are, Jesus wants to have the same conversation with you. I don't know your history. I don't know your past. Jesus knows all about you. He wants to look into your eyes and tell you:

I am going to start a new story with you. It's time to burn up the old storybook of betrayal, mess-ups, and bad choices. I am starting over with you. If you love me, I am about to start all over with you. Listen to me. Look at me. Speak for me. Be my hands. Be my feet.

Today you are probably at a point where you have to confess: I have not lived like Jesus. Like Peter, I have messed up. I am ready to love Jesus and start a new story.

MY PRAYER

Dear Jesus,

I am sorry I have not lived like you in my world. I have been a poor model. I have messed up. I want to start all over again. Jesus, I cannot do it in my strength. I need your help. I love you. I want to live like you, Jesus. In Jesus name. Amen.

[1] Read John 21

Section 3: I WITNESS

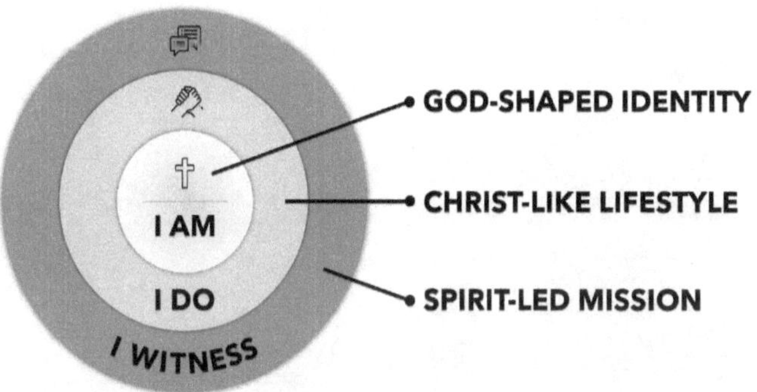

CHAPTER THIRTEEN

FRESH EXPERIENCE

The story is told about a man travelling by plane. He was seated next to a famous author. The man is overwhelmed at this great honour and opportunity. He repeatedly tells the author, 'You are my favourite author. How I wish, I had your latest book with me to get it autographed by you. It's in my personal library and I treasure the book.'

The famous author, eager to meet a fan, innocently asks him: 'What did you enjoy most in my latest book.'

The eager fan is suddenly silent because he hasn't ever read the book even though it was in his personal library.

There was a moment of awkward silence. The famous author kindly moved on and went on to explain his life journey and how this latest book was based on the challenges in his personal life.

The unfaithful fan goes home that night and climbs up the shelf and picks out the book and finishes the book through the night.

Knowing the author personally challenged him to eagerly read his words.

I invite you to a fresh experience with God that will draw you to study His word in deep reverence and awe.

A fresh experience with God will reveal who you are. Who He is will open your eyes to who you are.

A fresh experience with God will reveal what you are called to do. Who He is will open your eyes to what you are called to do.

Seek a fresh experience with God daily to grow healthy as a Christ-follower.

CHAPTER FOURTEEN

THE WATERSHED MOMENT

I want you to travel with me a little beyond the Book of James, and journey with me as we look at James the author and his personal journey.

Scholars tell us this is James, the brother of Jesus (being born to Mary and Joseph). He was not one of the twelve disciples of Jesus. James followed his brother Jesus' ministry from a distance. He did not choose to follow Jesus during his time on earth (John 7:5). Something happened to James around the time of Christ's crucifixion and resurrection. In fact, Jesus made a special appearance to James after his resurrection (1 Cor. 15:7). On the day of Pentecost in Acts, he is probably with the 120 waiting in the upper room.

By Acts 12, James was growing in his leadership in the first-century church. Peter, after he comes out of Prison, shares with the believers to share with James and the other brothers about his story.

In fact in Galatians, Apostle Paul goes on record to state James as one of the pillars of the church (2:9), along with Peter and John!

It was somewhere during this season, James writes the Book of James (AD45-48).

However, AD49 was a significant watershed moment for the Jesus-movement. Often referred to as the 'Jerusalem Council' recorded in Acts 15.

But, before we dive into Acts 15, let's recap our conversation so far in this book.

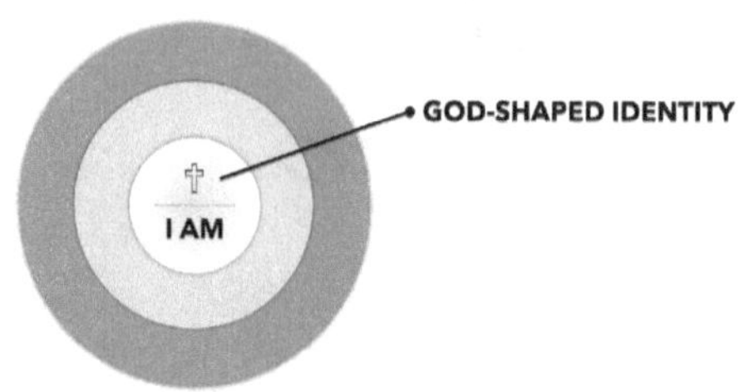

The first crucial element to be a healthy follower is a God-shaped identity.

Who I belong to shapes who I am

Where I stand shapes who I am

Who I am with shapes who I am

The second crucial element is a Jesus-like lifestyle.

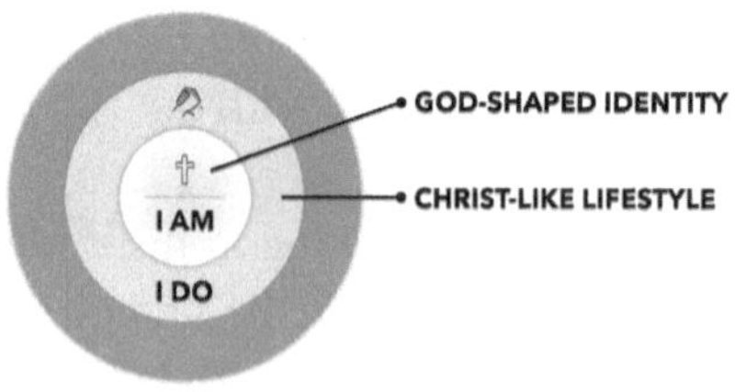

Ears – How I listen like Jesus

Eyes – How I see like Jesus

Tongue – How I speak like Jesus
Hands – How I act like Jesus
Feet – How I lead like Jesus
The final piece of being a healthy Christ-follower is living out a Spirit-led mission.

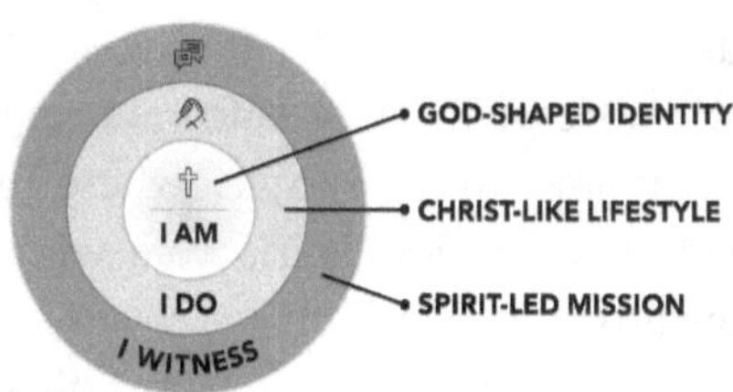

Well-known words of John Stott, *'Mission arises from the heart of God himself, and is communicated from his heart to ours. Mission is the global outreach of the global people of a global God.'*[1]

In Genesis 12: 1-3(NLT): God placed his awesome mission on Abraham's heart: *'Leave your native country...I will make you into a great nation...all the families on earth will be blessed through you'*

God's mission is unique. His heartbeat is for all families regardless of where they are.

In Matthew 28:18-20; Jesus places God's captivating mission on his disciples:

'...go and make disciples of all the nations...'

God's mission is really inclusive. His heartbeat is for all people everywhere.

In Acts 1:8(NLT): Jesus reveals that the Holy Spirit would spearhead God's grand mission

'But you will receive power when the Holy Spirit comes upon you. And you will be my witnesses, telling people about

me everywhere – In Jerusalem, throughout Judea, in Samaria, and to the ends of the earth'

God's mission is distinctive. It would be a Spirit-led mission to ignite a movement of Spirit-led witnesses.

How you witness is not about you leading the way. How you witness is dependent on you following the Holy Spirit where He leads.

A healthy movement is a spirit-led movement. A movement that follows the Holy Spirit where He leads.

When you follow the Holy Spirit, your witness takes on unique dimensions.

James in his letter presents the extraordinary qualities of a Spirit-led witness. It is Spirit-led because it is humanly not possible. Any witness which is engineered in the flesh or creatively crafted within the boundaries of your horizon, may incite, excite, ignite for a short season, but it is bound to fail in the long run. The spirit-led mission is always dependant on the Holy Spirit to make a difference in your world.

Well-known author, John Ortberg in his book *'When the game is over, it all goes back in the box'* talks about the Shadow mission.

'If we do not live our God-assigned mission, we will live what might be called a shadow mission, playing a game we were not meant to play...it consists of activities towards which I will gravitate if I allow my natural temptations and selfishness to take over. Everybody has a shadow mission'[2]

Most of us end up living a shadow mission because we are not following a Spirit-led mission. A Spirit-led mission always makes Jesus famous by drawing us to live like Jesus. A Spirit-led mission always draws us to cherish a God-shaped identity.

Acts 15 is a watershed moment. In a sense, the Holy Spirit was about to do something back then at that unique event, and nobody could have imagined how it was going to change the world. James, the author of one of the earliest letters, had no clue about how God was going to use him to launch a movement beyond Jews and Jerusalem and impact the entire globe.

AD 49 or AD 2021. God's mission must always be Spirit-led.

When they arrived in Jerusalem, Barnabas and Paul were welcomed by the whole church, including the apostles and elders. They reported everything God had done through them. But then some of the believers who belonged to the sect of the Pharisees stood up and insisted, "The Gentile converts must be circumcised and required to follow the law of Moses."

So the apostles and elders met together to resolve this issue.

When they had finished, James stood and said, "Brothers, listen to me. Peter has told you about the time God first visited the Gentiles to take from them a people for himself. ⋯

"And so my judgment is that we should not make it difficult for the Gentiles who are turning to God.'. (Acts 15:4-19 NLT)

I don't think James realised the depth of what he just spoke. Often we don't realise how profound are the words we speak until God creates history.

James by the power of the Holy Spirit was sowing the seeds for a Spirit-led healthy movement. These are three precious but impregnable seeds that have never changed over the last 2000 years.

- **God loves ALL** (Acts 15:14)

God loves ALL communities. God loves ALL people groups: Bengalis, Biharis, Tamilians, Telugus, Nagas, Mizos, Assamese, Oriya, North Indians, South Indians, Europeans, Pakistanis, Iranians, Chinese or the Mexican. God loves

ALL (If I failed to mention the name of your people group or language that's because in India alone there are over 2700 people groups and over 1700 languages– God loves all of them!).

Does God have favourites?

Yes, He has!

ALL are His favourites. All are special to Him.

A Spirit-led mission doesn't discriminate based on caste, creed, or community. A Spirit-led mission reveals the love of God to all.

- **God's Mission is for the WHOLE World**(Acts 15:16-18)

Nobody is outside the preview of God's mission. Regardless of our history, geography, or science: God's mission includes everyone. It includes your painful neighbour, difficult office colleague, messy hostel mate, intimidating office boss, and even your irritating classmate.

God wants the whole world to be shaped in His identity and discover the beauty of living a Jesus-like lifestyle.

- **I WITNESS – to be ALL Things to ALL People**(Acts 15:19-21)

The bottom line is that we should not make it difficult for anyone to experience the love of God.

Not our habits, nor our attitudes, or our activities. Anything that blocks people from experiencing the love of God should be deleted and trashed.

How can I be a witness? How can I be all things to all people at all times?

The Book of James doesn't specifically state exactly what it looks like when you have a Spirit-led mission. But James is a doing book and he pushes us beyond the boundaries of religious terminology. Being led by the Holy Spirit will have practical commitments of how you witness.

I am reminded of a little girl who got home from Sunday school, where she had been taught Matthew 5:16(NIV): *"Let your light so shine before men, that they may see your good works, and glorify your Father which is in heaven."* She asked her mother what the verse meant. Her mom lifted a candle and lit it and she whispered, "Well, it means that when you are good and kind and thoughtful and obedient, you are letting Christ's light shine in your life before all who know you and the candle shines brightly."

The very next week in Sunday school, the little girl got in a bit of a fight with another student and created somewhat of a scene. She created a scene to such an extent that the Sunday school teacher had to find her mother to get her settled down. Her mother was concerned when she got to the classroom and said, "Sweetie, don't you remember about letting your light shine for the Lord before people?" The girl blurted out, "Mom, I have blown myself out."

Most of the time, as Christ-followers we have blown out our candles and messed up our witness.

James presents before us six practical commitments we should make if we want to live as a witness in our community. As I share these practical commitments, I am going to place before you six specific challenges. Six things that I am going to dare you to do. It's a dare because you cannot do it in your strength unless the Holy Spirit empowers you and leads you.

[1] Stott, John R. W. *The Contemporary Christian: An Urgent Plea for Double Listening.* Leicester: Inter-Varsity Press, 1992. Print.

[2] Ortberg, John. *When the Game Is Over, It All Goes Back in the Box.* , 2015. Print.

CHAPTER FIFTEEN

CARING ACTS

December 20, 2020, *The New Yorker,* an influential US news magazine, had this interesting article titled: *An Advent Lament in the Pandemic.*[1] It covers how in the 2000 years of the Jesus-movement, Jesus-followers have been at the forefront of responding to pandemics, epidemics, plagues, outbreaks, poverty and how once again in 2020 they have done the same thing in responding to the Covid-19 pandemic. In fact, it concludes the article by quoting well-known scholar NT Wright from his new book, *God and the Pandemic,* that the witness of the church during suffering is: *"what the Church at its best has always believed and taught, and what the Church on the front lines has always practiced."*[2]

(James 1:27 NLT)*Pure and genuine religion in the sight of God the Father means caring for orphans and widows in their distress and refusing to let the world corrupt you.*

The first commitment of a witness that is Spirit-led is **CARING ACTS.**

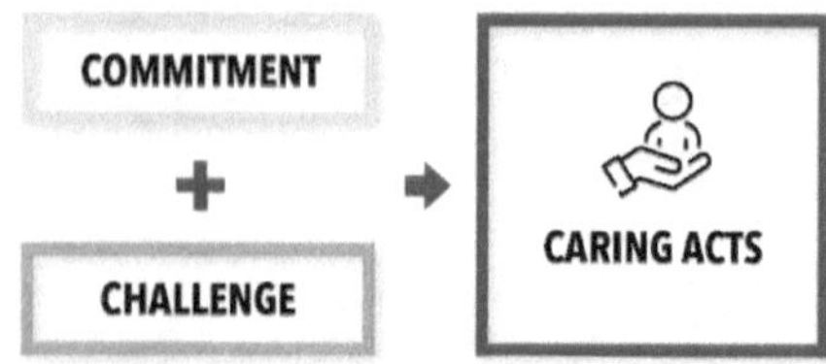

COMMITMENT

I witness when I care for the poor even when I don't have sufficient resources.

We don't have to wait until we have sufficient resources to care for the poor. We act even when we don't have enough.

Don't pray and wait for enough finances and resources before you can care for the orphans and widows around you. You will never have enough. But when you give with what you have, God blesses you with what you don't have.

Don't wait for an organisation or a structure to be set up before we can step out to do one caring act.

Can you and I choose to do just ONE caring act in ONE day? Every day.

Imagine the countless number of caring acts done daily around the world. We don't have to wait for the camera personnel to show up before we do one act of kindness.

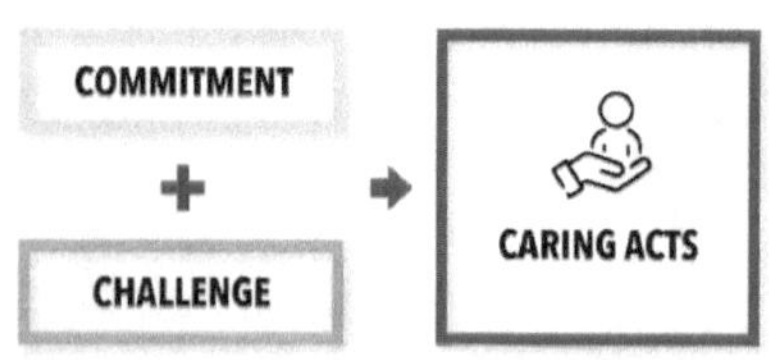

CHALLENGE
One caring act to one person daily silently and secretly.
(Don't post it on social media or tweet about it – just do it)
We are going to see a revolution of change across our city and nation.

---

[1] https://www.newyorker.com/news/daily-comment/an-advent-lament-in-the-pandemic

[2] Wright, N T. *God and the Pandemic: A Christian Reflection on the Coronavirus and Its Aftermath. ,* 2020. Print.

CHAPTER SIXTEEN

LIVING RIGHT

If you are wise and understand God's ways, prove it by living an honorable life, doing good works with the humility that comes from wisdom (James 3:13 NLT)

The second commitment of a Spirit-led vibrant life of witness is

LIVING RIGHT.

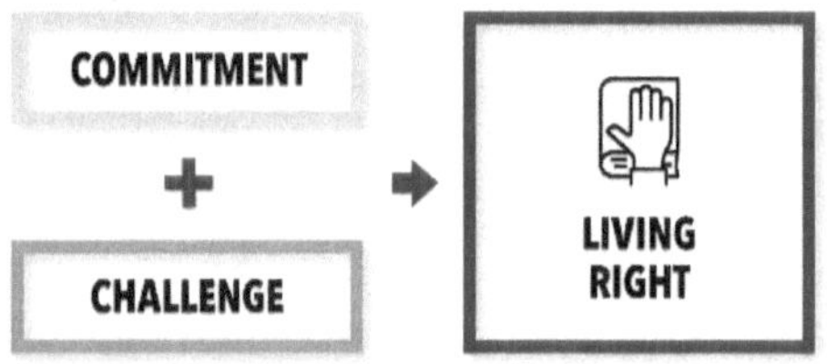

COMMITMENT

I witness when I live a life of integrity even when I am surrounded by the most dishonest circumstances.

One of the biggest excuses for not living right is the reality of the unfair world around us. They are all living wrong. Why should I bother to live right?

Turn to the newspaper. Turn on your newsfeed. Turn on the TV. Turn to your friends. Turn to your leaders. Turn everywhere. Nobody is living right. Why bother to live right?

In fact, even God turned on His newsfeed in heaven and had the same realization: *Psalm 14:3(NLT): 'All have turned away, all have become corrupt; there is no one who does good, not even one'*

Living right is impossible unless you are led by the Spirit.

Paul in his letter to the Galatians in 5: 16 and 25(NLT):

So I say, let the Holy Spirit guide your lives. Then you won't be doing what your sinful nature craves.

Since we are living by the Spirit, let us follow the Spirit's leading in every part of our lives.

The familiar words of one of my favourite songs make us realize we cannot live right without God's help.

I need you more
More than yesterday
I need you more
More than words can say
I need you more
Than ever before
I need you Lord
I need you Lord
More than the air I breath
More than the song I sing
More than the next heartbeat
More than anything.
And, Lord, as the time goes by
I'll be by your side
'Cause I never want to go back
To my old life.

The Lord is always by our side. The key to living right: *Will I always be by the Lord's side?*

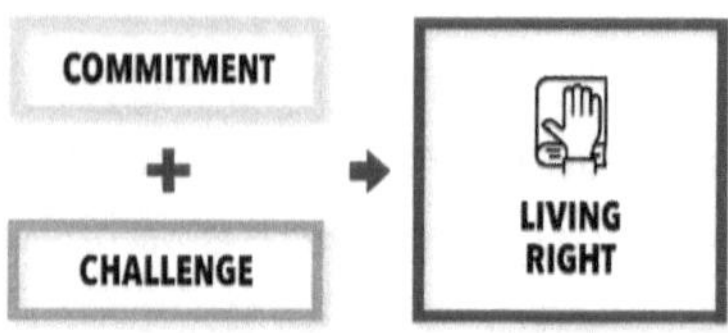

CHALLENGE

Before you make any major or minor decision, will you whisper a prayer: Lord, I want to honour you in this decision?

CHAPTER SEVENTEEN

OVERCOMING SATAN

So humble yourselves before God. Resist the devil, and he will flee from you. (James 4:7)

The third commitment to a Spirit-led vibrant life of witness is

OVERCOMING SATAN.

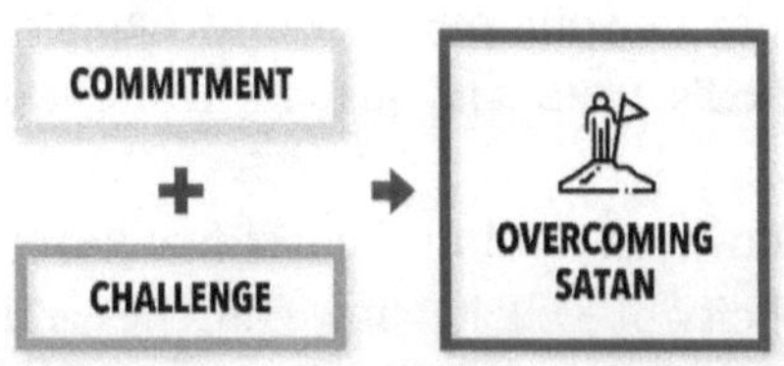

COMMITMENT

I witness when I resist the devil at all times.

In Bengal(State in India), Satan is found in almost every neighbourhood.

That's because parents keep calling their mischievous kids – *'Shaitan (Satan), come here'!*

While we have been busy calling people, 'Satan' and 'devils', Satan has been busy with bigger purposes:

- Getting us to break our families
- Deactivating us with destructive habits
- Corrupting our hearts and hands to sell small girls into sex slavery(In the last twenty-four hours nearly 180 girls have been sold into sex trafficking all over India[1])
- Poisoning our relationships with jealousy, prejudice, and envy
- Getting us so busy with our world that we have forgotten God's Word

Your greatest witness is living a life in total submission to God. The only vaccine to a devil-intoxicated world is a Jesus-obsessed lifestyle.

Overcoming Satan's agenda in your private life happens when you walk in submission to God daily. Overcoming Satan's agenda in your public world happens when you speak out God's truth and justice in the worst possible scenario.

It has been wonderful in the last few years to notice in my beautiful city of Kolkata, how churches and NGOs have come together in prayer, acts of justice, public awareness campaigns to push back the works of Satan across our city and state. There is much more to be done, but as we come together, our beloved City of Joy will experience what the psalmist calls: *taking away our clothes of mourning and clothing us with joy!(Psalm 30:11)*

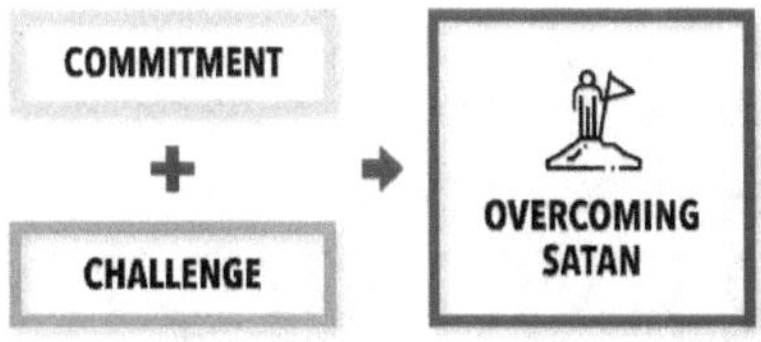

CHALLENGE

Highlight ONE act of injustice in your community and make it a matter of passionate prayer and wise action.

[1] https://timesofindia.indiatimes.com/city/hyderabad/every-8-minutes-a-girl-child-goes-missing-in-india-how-long-will-we-keep-sacrificing-our-children/articleshow/60279189.cms

CHAPTER EIGHTEEN

PRESSING ON

Dear brothers and sisters, be patient as you wait for the Lord's return. Consider the farmers who patiently wait for the rains in the fall and in the spring. They eagerly look for the valuable harvest to ripen. You, too, must be patient. Take courage, for the coming of the Lord is near. (James 5:7-8 NLT)

The fourth commitment of a Spirit-led vibrant witness is

PRESSING ON

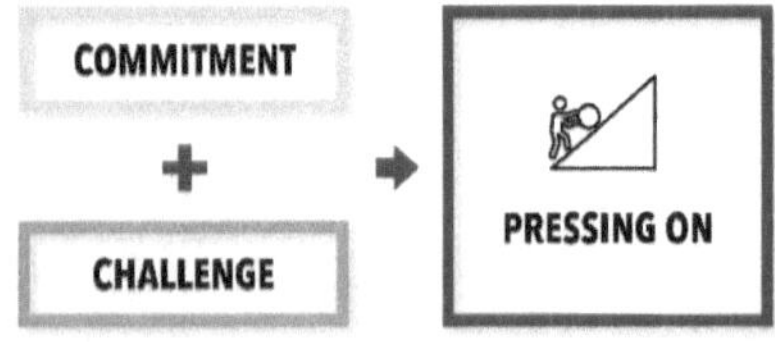

COMMITMENT

I witness when I walk in endurance even when I feel like giving up.

One of the biggest heartaches of the Jesus-movement in the twenty-first century is the tendency to give up when we are not happy with the immediate situation.

Immediate situation sadly in most cases is quite frivolous:

- We give up following Christ because the worship team did not sing my favourite song
- We give up following Christ because the Pastor forgot to wish me on my anniversary
- We give up following Christ because I was not chosen for the choir
- We give up following Christ because my favourite seat was given to a new guest in the service
- We give up on life because my picture on social media had only fifty likes while my classmate got seventy-five likes
- We give up on life because 'she' did not respond to my Whatsapp message

I feel, *one of the greatest visible acts of your witness is being faithful regardless of everything that crumbles around you.*

Faithful to God.

Faithful to your commitments.

Faithful to the church.

You may not become famous. You may not make it to any committee. Your name may never get mentioned anywhere. You keep pressing on.

You are patient. You are enduring. Because your eyes are fixed on Jesus, the Faithful One. Your eyes are fixed on Jesus, waiting for His return. Your eyes are fixed on Jesus, to set right things which have gone wrong in your life.

The founding pastor of the Assembly of God Church, Kolkata, Pastor Mark Buntain – had two words in response when anybody asked him, 'How are you doing?'

'Pressing on' was Pastor Buntain's vibrant response.

Pressing on is a powerful form of witness.

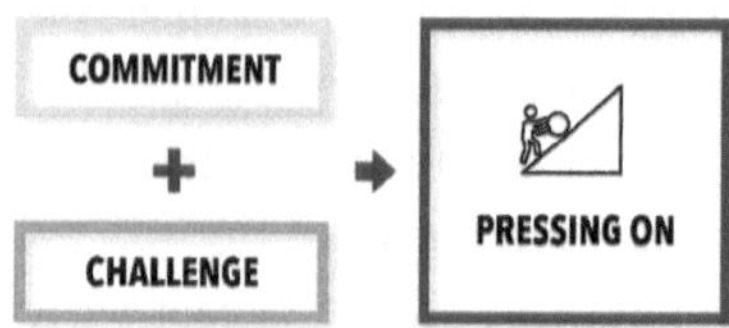

CHALLENGE:

Find one person you trust (a friend or pastor) and share the one moment you were ready to give up because you were offended. (Take time to receive prayer from your friend).

CHAPTER NINETEEN

PRAYING POWER

Are any of you suffering hardships? You should pray. Are any of you happy? You should sing praises. Are any of you sick? You should call for the elders of the church to come and pray over you, anointing you with oil in the name of the Lord. Such a prayer offered in faith will heal the sick, and the Lord will make you well. (James 5:13-15 NLT)

The fifth commitment of a Spirit-led vibrant witness is **PRAYING POWER.**

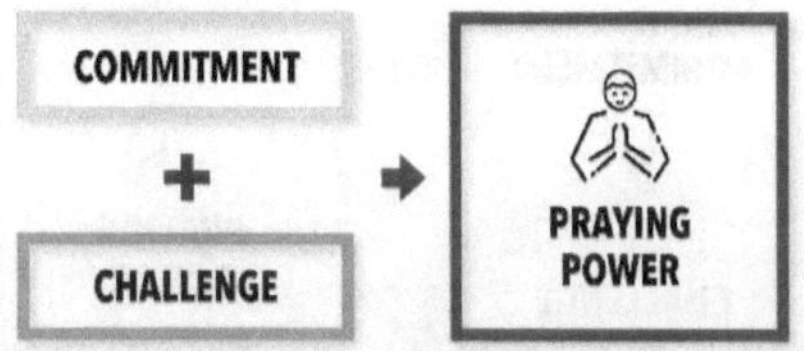

COMMITMENT

I witness when I pray and expect miracles to happen.

If I were to pause now and allow you to write down: one story of a miracle you experienced as somebody prayed with you.

I wonder what your story would look like.

With impossible situations, we have walked into the presence of God. As we prayed or a prayer team stood around you, you experienced a miracle immediately or over a few days or in a few months. Many of us have experienced the power of prayer.

Today, are you in need of a miracle? It's time not to give up. It's time to gather together with your church family. Pray in faith and believe for a touch from Jesus.

We value the wonderful ministry of our medical doctors and all our friends in the healthcare community. We pray for our doctors to excel and provide the best care possible. But we also pray for miracles to happen even when there is no hope.

Pastor Patrick Joseph, the Senior Associate Pastor at The Assembly of God Church, Kolkata, made this profound statement that captures the essence of prayer: 'EVERYTHING by prayer' but not 'EVERYTHING and then prayer'

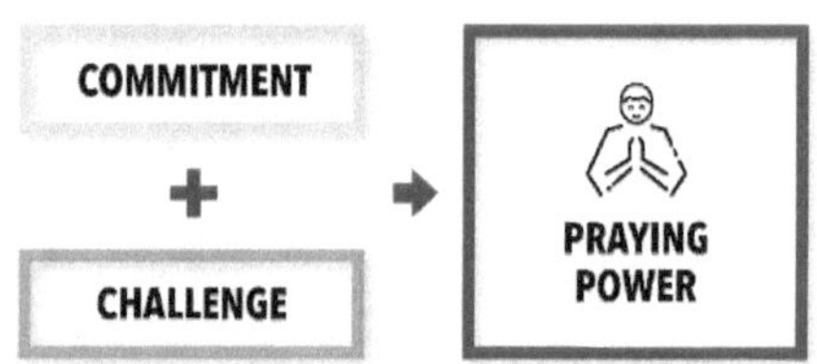

CHALLENGE

Make prayer your default first response when faced with a difficult situation, and not the last response.

CHAPTER TWENTY

LOVING WELCOME

My dear friends, if you know people who have wandered off from God's truth, don't write them off. Go after them. Get them back and you will have rescued precious lives from destruction and prevented an epidemic of wandering away from God. (James 5:19-20 MSG)

The final commitment of a Spirit-led witness is a **LOVING WELCOME:**

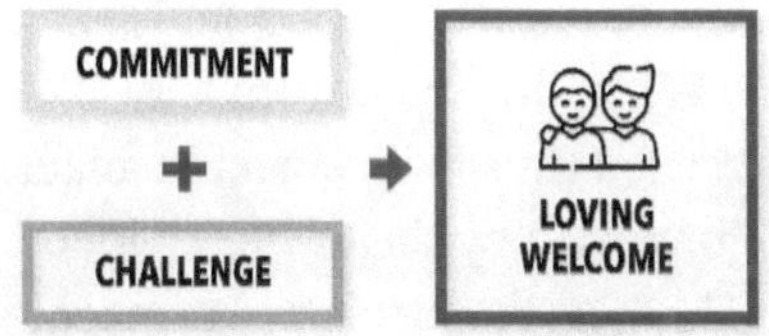

COMMITMENT

I witness when I welcome back home God's weakest child.

We are all weak, and we are all prone to wander away. By God's grace, we find ourselves in God's family. While there are many more that the enemy has blinded and drawn them far from home.

Our posture is to be like the waiting father in Luke 15. Waiting and praying and doing whatever it takes to celebrate the feeble steps a person is taking as he seeks to return home.

Most of the time our witness has been like the elder brother. Grumbling and complaining that the brother who has returned home has flooded the social media newsfeed.

Once upon a time, all of us were like the younger brother, and somebody took the time to welcome us home.

Once upon a time, all of us were lost, Jesus welcomed us home.

Spirit-led witness means we give up on nobody. Nobody is far from God's love. Nobody is beyond the purview of Jesus' nail-pierced hands. Will you be the extended hands of Jesus?

We are all weak. The words of this famous hymn, *Come thou fount*, make that your daily prayer.

Prone to wander, Lord, I feel it;
Prone to leave the God I love:
Take my heart, oh, take and seal it
With Thy Spirit from above.
Rescued thus from sin and danger,
Purchased by the Savior's blood,
May I walk on earth a stranger,
As a son and heir of God.

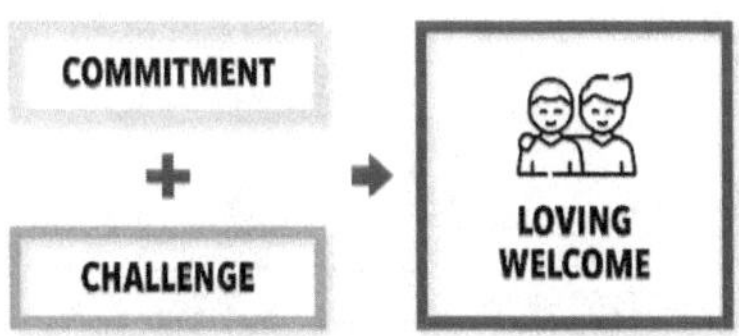

CHALLENGE

Write down and pray daily for ONE friend who is no longer in God's family. Pray for opportunities to connect with him/ her.

CHAPTER TWENTY-ONE

LIKE JESUS...

I want to place before you one of the most moving moments that have impacted me.

Huddled up in a room. Doors locked from inside. Total Lockdown. Late, one Sunday evening. Few men sat talking to each other. Softly and hushed up, they were really scared about the future. They sat as men who had no dreams. No hope. No direction.

Suddenly, miraculously stood among them the epitome of Hope, Life, and Truth. He lifted his hands and showed them the wounds in his hands and his side. Then He said something which,I believe, holds the essence of what it means to be a healthy follower.

'As the Father has sent me, so I am sending you' (John 20:21 NLT)

These eleven words capture for me the captivating Spirit-led mission.

Jesus was speaking his final words. His closing comments to his disciples. He brings together who He is and what He is calling us to do.

As the Father has sent me:

I am.

I live a God-shaped identity.

I belong to God and I am designed to be like my Father.

I obey His every instruction.

I stand strong in the power of God's word, God's wisdom.

I am with God and I have overcome the power of the fallen nature, the world, and the devil.

As the Father has sent me.

I do.

I am sent into this world to model how you are to live.

Look at my life.

Look at how I lived?

My words. My works. My wonders.

As the father has sent me, I am sending you

I witness.

I am sending you now into the world.

On this Spirit-led mission.

To flesh out. Caring acts, live right, overcome Satan, pressing on, praying power, and loving welcome.

Today Jesus stands before you.

He looks into your eyes – *Peace be with you - As the Father has sent me, so I am sending you.*

You are sent into your world to be like Jesus in your world.

You are:

- A home-maker - *You will live like Jesus within your sphere of influence*
- A young man or a young lady - *You will live like Jesus in your college or school*
- A young professional - *You will live like Jesus in your workplace*
- A sincere seeker - *You will discover who this Jesus is*
- A pastor or leader - *You will lead like Jesus to all those who follow you.*

It is no accident where you are.

God has placed you where you are so that the world might see Jesus through you.

You are the only Jesus the world will ever see. My prayer is that you will:

- *Pursue a God-shaped identity*
- *Pursue a Jesus-like lifestyle*
- *Pursue a Spirit-led mission*

MY PRAYER

Dear Jesus,

I commit to follow you all the way. I desire an identity shaped by the heavenly father. I desire to live like you in my world. I desire to be led by the Spirit to be a vibrant witness. Here I am. Use me for your glory. In Jesus name. Amen.

Pay It Forward

In 1999, Catherine Ryan Hyde's novel *Pay It Forward* was published and then adapted into a film in 2000 with the same name. In Ryan Hyde's book and movie, it is described as a commitment to do three good deeds for others in response to a good deed that one receives. Such good deeds should accomplish things that the other person cannot accomplish on their own. In this way, the practice of helping one another can spread geometrically through society, at a ratio of three to one, creating a social movement with an impact of making the world a better place.

I have been the recipient of the biggest and best act of love. Jesus. He died for me. I live for Him.

How can I pay it forward?

First, is the book. I have been mentored and equipped by so many great authors in my life's journey. I am thankful for each of them. This book is my feeble attempt to invest in the next generation. *Dear Next Gen, I believe in you and excited for the amazing possibilities of how you can be a dynamic movement of Christ-followers.*

Second, is my gratefulness to my friends and family. The whole journey of writing a book is never a solo experience. I am grateful to friends who graciously invested their time and gifts to make this journey possible.

- A group of 20 praying friends who have prayed for every critical step in my life and ministry. You especially prayed for my journey with this book. *Thank you so much!*
- The AGK pastoral team and colleagues. You have been a

vital cog to shape my perspectives and experiences on what a healthy Christ-movement looks like. *Thank you so much!*

- Leaders, mentors and friends of the Jesus-movement in Kolkata. I get to hang out with you in so many events and locations. I have learnt a lot from you. *Thank you so much!*

- The excellent support team behind this book project. Jilian Gomes, who meticulously proof-read the entire manuscript to ensure there was no grammatical errors or typos. Johns George, my close friend who willingly made himself available to design this entire book. *Thank you so much!*

- Dr. Ivan Satyavrata, my Senior Pastor and mentor. Pastor Ivan planted the seed of the idea for this book, early in 2021. In spite of his busy schedule, he was always available to give guidance and input towards this book project. *Thank you so much!*

- My wife and my two sons. All that I am, I do and I witness is painstakingly filtered by them. *Thank you so much!*

Thirdly, invest into AG Care[1]. I am blessed that my sons go to school. I am blessed that my family is able to have at least three meals a day. I am blessed that we are able to drink clear drinking water. But a large percentage of children in India don't have access to go to school. They are glad to be able to eat even one meal. Clean drinking water is a luxury. That's why through AG CARE, I want to pay it forward and make a difference in my world. That's why when one person buys this book, the proceeds of it goes towards AG Care.

Are you willing to pay it forward?

[1] AG CARE is engaged in various social endeavors including a child sponsorship program (The Cry of India), a daily feeding program, homes for the orphaned, and a biosand clean water initiative, among others, to serve the needs of the poorest of the poor in Kolkata and other parts of West Bengal and Eastern India. The author is personally invested in this social endeavour. For more details, visit the website: https://agcareindia.org/

Ag Care

(from the AGCARE website: https://agcareindia.org/)

AG Care is engaged in various social endeavors including a child sponsorship program (The Cry of India), a daily feeding program, homes for the orphaned, and a biosand clean water initiative, among others, to serve the needs of the poorest of the poor in Kolkata and other parts of West Bengal and Eastern India.

India is a country known for her rich history and wealth of cultural diversity, beauty and spirit. Sadly, India is also home to some of the poorest people in the world. AG Care is committed to recognising and responding to the suffering of these people in the city of Kolkata and other needy regions of North and East India.

THE CRY OF INDIA

"India is the youngest nation in the world with more than 50% of India below the age of 18" Despite major efforts in India, the number of children who are not in school remains high. Gender disparities in education persist, far more girls than boys failing to complete primary school. The education system of India faces a shortage of resources, schools, classrooms and teachers.

Our child care service (The Cry of India) facilitates sponsorship for over 5,000 needy children in 57 schools across East India. These children receive quality education in our schools, a nutritious mid-day meal, and have access to basic health care, giving them an opportunity to rise to their full potential and to pursue a bright future.

In an effort to meet these challenges, AG Care provides education to over 10,000 girls and boys in three different language mediums: English, Hindi, and Bengali. Our education network includes 4 English schools, 10 vernacular schools, 1 vocational school, and 1 junior teacher training college. Our schools are spread across the length and breadth of West Bengal and are located at Kolkata, Haldia, Purulia, Ashokenagar, Bongaon, Guma, Maslandapur, Dum Dum, Keorapukur, Kestopur, and Taherpur.

FEEDING

Despite economic growth and self-sufficiency in food grains production, high levels of poverty, food insecurity and malnutrition continue to persist in India. Home to a quarter of all undernourished people worldwide, one in every three malnourished children in the world lives in India. About 50% of all childhood deaths are attributed to malnutrition. People living on the streets of Kolkata endure some of the most severe economic and material hardships in the world.

6 days a week, AG Care provides a nourishing meal to 10,000 children and adults of needy families through 7 access points at Park Street, Bosetala, Bantala, Kantatala, Bamanghatta, Karaidanga, and Bhojerhat, as well as 10 schools in and around Kolkata. Our dedicated catering service cooks more than 1000 kilos of rice every day!

BIOSAND FILTER

At least half the population of India lacks access to basic sanitation facilities and well maintained water supply. This creates a very high risk of microbial contamination (bacteria, viruses, amoeba), causing diarrhoea. In India, diarrhoea alone causes more than 1,600 deaths daily. Children weakened by frequent diarrhoea episodes are more vulnerable to malnutrition infections like pneumonia. Diarrhoea and worm infection are two major health conditions that affect school age children impacting their learning abilities. AG Care is committed to combating disease in India by providing clean water to families and children. Through our clean water initiative, 3000 biosand filters have been installed and are being used in 34 villages over Jharkhand and West Bengal, providing safe drinking water and improving life for thousands.

Why I Recommend...

Rev. Dr. Jacob Mathew begins with Christians' God-shaped Identity; moving from that sure foundation to a Christ-like Lifestyle, he then addresses a Spirit-led Mission. God the Father, Son and Holy Spirit are intimately invested in creating healthy conditions for healthy believers. Dr. Mathew invites people on an every-day faith journey that changes individuals, families, and communities alike.

Dr. Ellen L. Marmon, Ph.D., Doctor of Ministry. Director, Asbury Theological Seminary.

This book is a creative, vividly imaginative and highly readable summary of the message of James' epistle. It is also an earnest invitation from a thoughtful pastor for Christ-followers of this generation to grow out of a superficial `lip-service' faith into healthy mature disciples.But more than that, it is a passionate call from the heart of one who longs to see [in his own words] "...a greater movement of vibrant fresh flourishing genre of healthy Christ-followers" emerge in this generation.

Dr. Ivan Satyavrata, AG Church, Kolkata, India

Dr. Jacob Mathew in his book answers an important question of how to be a healthy Christ-follower. Using the book of James he outlines three key ideas of "I am, I do and I witness." I love the way he combines solid theology with practical application.

Dr. Paul Marzahn, Crossroads Church Multi-Site, Minnesota, USA

Dr. Jacob Mathew is well respected for his leadership as the Regional Youth Director for the Assemblies of God of North India. He is able to inspire youth to reach their God-given potential. In his book 'I am. I Do. I Witness' Dr.

Mathew portrays practical truths from the Book of James on what it means to be a healthy Christ-follower. He sums it this way: "Who I am with, shapes who I am" and "Who I am shapes what I do." Though it is simple in it's reading, it challenges you to discover your identity and emulate our Lord in our every day life.

Rev. Valson Varghese
National Youth Director, AG India
Co-Chair, Next Gen. Commission
World Assemblies of God Fellowship

About The Author

Jacob Mathew serves on the leadership team at The Assembly of God Church, Kolkata, India. Over the last twenty years, he has been involved in a wide range of activities that has changed his own life (and hopefully the life of people around him). He doesn't really love to talk a lot. But his role unfortunately requires him to talk quite a bit. He is often considered creative, because of the creative people he is privileged to serve with.

He had to go to school and college for several years of his life. More than the degrees he received at these institutions, he cherishes the life-changing experiences that have shaped his life and ministry. St. Xavier's College, Kolkata (with Bachelors in Commerce) taught him the value of waking up very early in the morning. Centre for Global Leadership Development, Bangalore (at SABC with Masters in Divinity) shaped him to treasure the value of healthy relationships in a faith-community. Asbury Theological Seminary, Kentucky (with Doctor in Ministry) formed a holistic journey of healthy habits with deep devotion.

He is married to Neena and have two sons, Josiah and Joash. Literally, that changed his life. And, they continue to change him.

He learns a lot when he goes on long walks(without his Smartphone); sitting in a coffee shop(reading a novel); watching a movie (even the animation movies with his sons); and, logging into social media(more than he would like to!).